YOU'LL LA

What's a Po

Two Band-A

————————

Why did the cannibal rush over to the cafeteria?

He heard children were half price.

————————

What do you call a guy with no arms and no legs who's in a pot with a bunch of vegetables?

Stu.

————————

How do they play strip poker in a nudist colony?

With a pair of tweezers.

————————

What are two fingers to a girl with bulimia?

Dessert.

INCREDIBLY GROSS JOKES

VOLUME XV

Julius Alvin

ZEBRA BOOKS
KENSINGTON PUBLISHING CORP.

ZEBRA BOOKS are published by

Kensington Publishing Corp.
475 Park Avenue South
New York, NY 10016

Zebra and the Z logo are trademarks of Kensington Publishing Corp.

First Printing: November, 1993

Printed in the United States of America

DEDICATION

To my brother Marty,
for his sense of humor and
a sense of responsibility
that far surpasses mine.

TABLE OF CONTENTS

Chapter One:

Gross Racial and Ethnic Jokes

Did you hear about the girl who was expelled from school for eating a Polish sausage?

The Polack was expelled, too.

———————————

Why do black men cry after sex?

Mace.

How can you tell the guy you met in a bar is Polish?

He keeps a wallet in his condom.

A guy walked into a bar and saw his Polish friend downing double after double. He walked over and said, "Stash, what's wrong?"

The Polack said, "I think my wife is screwing around on me."

"How do you know?"

"This afternoon I was walking down Main Street when I saw somebody with a coat exactly like hers walking into a porno theater with a guy."

The friend asked, "Why didn't you go in and make sure if it was her or not?"

The Polack said, "I already saw the picture."

Why did the Polack fail his biology test?

He thought bacteria was the rear entrance to a cafeteria.

The Polack walked into the doctor's office and said, "Doc, I want you to examine my finger tips."

"Why your finger tips?"

"I don't feel well."

The Polack walked into the doctor's office holding his stomach and said, "I have this awful stomach ache ever since I ate clams last night."

The doctor said, "Seafood is often the cause of food poisoning. Tell me, did the clams look or smell funny when you opened the shells?"

The Polack said, "You mean, you're supposed to open the shells?"

Did you hear about the Polack who was killed by a headache?

He put his head through a window to see if the *pane* would disappear.

The Polack walked into the doctor's office and said, "Doc, I have this problem when I'm in bed with my wife. I start to stick it in, and my eyesight gets all blurry. By the time I'm all the way in, I can't see a thing."

"That's strange," the doctor said. "Why don't you let me see it?"

So the Polack stuck out his tongue.

———————

The doctor walked back into the office where the Italian woman was sitting and said, "Mrs. Masucci, that wasn't a urine sample you gave me. That was apple juice."

The woman bolted out of her chair and screamed, "Outta my way. I gotta call my son's school!"

———————

What's Puerto Rican foreplay?

Yelling, "Lose the pants or I'll cut you."

The Polish girl walked into the courthouse and said, "I met a guy in a bar last night and took him home. Now I want to sue him."

The clerk said, "I don't think we can help you. This is Small Claims Court."

The Polish girl said, "I'm in the right place. He was a lot smaller than he claimed."

The Chinese couple were on a ship bound for America. Finally, they spotted San Francisco's Golden Gate Bridge. The husband turned to the wife and asked, "Do you know what that means?"

She replied. "Yes, I do. Now you'll spend your days doing laundry and at night, I'll be on top."

How can you tell if a woman's a WASP?

She even rides her Kotex side-saddle.

Did you hear about the rich redneck who bought a new house?

His relatives helped him take the wheels off it.

_____

What's a Polish *hors d'oeuvre*?

Spam on a saltine.

_____

What's the definition of a redneck?

A guy whose idea of entertainment is sitting outside watching the bug zapper.

Why is it more expensive to go to the junior prom in Harlem than it is in the suburbs?

Girls have to pay extra to leave their kids at the day-care center.

_____

Why was the Polack's Thanksgiving dinner ruined?

He ran out of ketchup.

_____

A guy ran into his Polish friend and said, "I hear congratulations are in order. I understand you're getting married."

"Yeah," the Polack said. "But these wedding preparations are killing me."

"You mean sending out invitations, ordering the cake, that kind of stuff?"

"Nah," the Polack said. "I mean hitting every men's room in town to erase 'For a great blow-job, call Veronica.'"

Why did the redneck father walk his son to school every day?

They were in the same grade.

_____

Why do rednecks love family reunions?

It's a chance to meet women.

_____

What's the difference between a black kid and a white kid?

A black kid is always wondering how they keep the subways so clean.

_____

What's a Polish bikini?

Two Band-Aids and two corks.

Why did the Italian wife buy a glass diaphragm?

She wanted a picture window in the rumpus room.

———————

If you walked into a room and discovered an Iraqi woman naked, what would be the first thing she'd cover?

The goat.

A Polish guy walked into a coffee shop one day and ran into an old high school friend. He asked, "What are you doing now?"

The friend said, "I've been studying at M.I.T. Now I hold a prestigious position as a nuclear physicist."

The Polack said, "Well, I got a great job, too. I'm with the sanitation department."

The scientist smirked. "How can you compare being a garbage man with being a physicist. Why, I know how to split atoms."

"So?" the Polack replied. "I can break wind."

What's a WASP?

A guy who goes to a porno movie and only raises his eyebrows.

What's the best-selling Greek lipstick?

Preparation H.

_____

Why do Polish women cook dinner with their panties off?

To keep the flies away from the food.

The young black teen kept pestering his father for a car. Finally, his old man said, "Boy, you can't get a car until you be a man. Can your dick reach your asshole?"

"No," the young man said.

"Then you ain't gettin' no car."

A couple years passed. On his eighteenth birthday, the black kid went back to his father and said, "Can I get a car now?"

"Does your dick reach your asshole?"

"Not quite."

The father said, "Then you can't have no car."

On his twenty-first birthday, the young black man rushed into the house and said, "Pop, I'm ready for that car. My dick finally reaches my asshole!"

"Good," his father said. "Now, go fuck yourself!"

The San Francisco streetwalker was displaying her charms when a young Chinese guy came up to her. He didn't speak any English, but they began to haggle in sign language. It was very late and he was persistent, so she finally agreed to $50 for the night. She led him towards her usual hotel, but he pointed to another establishment across the street. She finally gave in.

Soon they were in bed. After a vigorous screw, he leaped out of bed and headed for the shower. She was just about to fall asleep when he was beside her in bed with another raging hard-on.

They fucked again, and again, he leaped out of bed. This time she was asleep when she was awakened by another rigid organ. "Oh, no," she groaned, "I can't believe this guy." Her nightmare went on for another two hours. Finally, exhausted, she dragged herself out of bed, saying, "If a shower can do it for this guy, maybe it will do it for me."

Then she opened the bathroom door and saw five Chinese guys in the shower.

A guy walked into a bar, ordered a drink, and said, "Hey, anyone here know how you can tell if an Irish guy found a $20 bill? Smell his breath!"

A couple guys laughed, but a big brute at the bar came over to the comedian and said, "Mac, I'm Irish. And I don't like Irish jokes. So if you want to keep all your teeth, don't tell any more jokes that involve me or my people."

"You mean, you want to hear a joke that doesn't involve you in any way at all?"

"That's right," the Irishman said.

"Okay," the guy said, "your wife is pregnant."

What's a Puerto Rican girl's idea of birth control?

Making it to the delivery room.

What do Japanese men do when they have erections?

Vote.

The guy walked in the front door and said, "I'm horny and I want to fuck a Polish girl. That woman lying over there, is she Polish?"

The woman said, "I'm going to have to ask you to leave."

The guy said, "What? Are you prejudiced or something? I just want to fuck that Polish girl over there."

The woman asked, "By any chance, are you Polish?"

"Yeah," the guy said. "How did you know?"

"Because this is a funeral home."

What's a Puerto Rican birth certificate?

The refund letter from the condom company.

———————————

Why do Polacks make the best secret agents?

Even under torture they can't remember what they were assigned to do.

———————————

What do you get when you cross a JAP and an elephant?

The world's most expensive nose job.

A Jewish man walks into a jewelry store. He says, "I want to buy a present for my wife." He points to a silver crucifix and asks, "How much?"

"Six hundred dollars," replies the salesman.

"How much would it be without the acrobat?"

———————

An Irish woman and an Italian woman lived in the same tenement building. One day the Irish woman bet her friend that she could stick her ass out the window longer.

The Italian woman agreed, so they both sat on the sill with their ponderous posteriors hanging out. Finally, after a couple of hours, the Irish woman's husband came home and asked what was going on. The wife told him about the bet.

"That's fine and dandy. But I need a blowjob," the Irishman said.

"But I'll lose the bet."

"You give me a blowjob and I'll stick my ass out the window. That Italian woman won't know the difference."

So they changed places. A few minutes later, the Italian woman looked over and saw a pair of balls hanging below her friend's ass. "Molly!" she screamed. "You betta get your ass inside. Your guts are starting to spill out!"

What do French women do for their men at Christmas?

They use flavored Tampax.

———

What's different about a Harlem school newspaper?

It has an obituary column.

———

How can you tell a teacher has a Puerto Rican class?

She's got graffiti under her skirt.

What do they do in biology class in Harlem?

They dissect a janitor.

Why do they have recess in Harlem schools?

To evacuate the wounded.

What's another way to recognize a Puerto Rican school?

The textbooks are in spray paint.

What do they study in sex education in a Harlem school?

Whoever they drag in off the street.

_____

What's the difference between a pig and a pervert?

A pig farts in her movie seat; a pervert goes over and smells the seat after the show.

_____

Why can't women work in Polish bakeries?

The government's afraid of yeast infections.

The young hillbilly married a girl from the next valley and took her into the mountains for a honeymoon. He'd only been gone one day, however, when he angrily stormed back home to his Pappy.

"Where's your bride?" Pappy asked.

"I done shot her."

"Why?"

"She were a virgin, Paw."

Pappy replied, "You done the right thing, son. If she weren't good enough for her own kin, she ain't good enough for you."

What's a redneck's idea of a quiet evening?

Gagging his thirteen-year-old sister before he ties her to the bed and fucks her.

How can you tell a Polish girl has bulimia?

After she eats, she sticks two fingers up her ass to shit it all out.

How can you tell if a woman is a JAP?

The circles under her eyes are Arctic.

Why did the redneck go out every night and jerk off the dog?

To feed his cat.

A company president decides he needs a new building, so he calls some contractors in to submit bids. The first guy he talks to is Polish. "You've had a chance to look at the plans," he says. "How much will it cost to build?"

"Two million," replies the Polish contractor. "One million for materials, one million for labor."

The company president thanks the Polack, and calls in an Italian contractor.

The Italian's bid is four million. "How would you break that down?" the company president asks. "Two million for materials, two million for labor," the Italian replies.

The company president dismisses him, then calls in the third man, a Jewish contractor. "How much are you bidding?" the president asks.

"Six million."

"Six million? That's very high. How do you break that down?"

"It's simple," said the Jewish contractor. "Two million for me, two million for you, and two million for the Polack."

Why did the Polack run out of the bullfights?

When the matador screamed "Toro!", he went home to get his lawn mower.

———————

Why did the Polack woman think she was having an illegal abortion?

The doctor was wearing a mask.

———————

What's a Polish handjob?

A girl sucks your fingers.

What's the difference between blacks and radial tires?

Radial tires don't sing spirituals when you put chains on them.

_____

Did you hear about the Mississippi town that couldn't decide between starting a chapter of the Ku Klux Klan and organizing a baseball league?

They compromised by hunting down blacks and beating them to death with bats.

_____

What's the first thing a WASP wife does after sex?

Moves.

What kind of sexual lubricant do racists use?

KKK-Y jelly.

———————————

Why did the Polack go to the Chinese Hand Laundry?

He'd just beat off, and he wanted to get cleaned up.

———————————

What did the Polack do when he wanted music to dance in his head?

Bought a headband.

Why do Polacks love girls with big noses?

Easy pickings.

_____

Did you hear about the Polack who opened a topless bar?

A week of rain bankrupted him.

The Polish government decided to enhance its prestige by building the longest bridge in the world for an underdeveloped country. So Polish engineers constructed a span all the way over the Sahara Desert.

Instead of prestige, however, all the Polish government got was ridicule. They decided to send a team of engineers to Africa to tear down the structure. But when the bridge demolition team arrived, they reported they couldn't touch the structure.

"Your orders are to go ahead and blow it up," shouted the president of Poland.

"Okay," said the head engineer. "But we're gonna kill a couple thousand Italians who are fishing off it."

———————

What's the definition of a virgin Bosnian soldier?

One who hasn't raped his first ten women.

Did you hear about the Polish baby who was hurt at his baptism?

Someone flushed.

––––––––––––––––

Did you hear about the Japanese factory that painted all its robots black?

The next day, the robots were all in the john smoking dope.

––––––––––––––––

What do you call a 200-pound Russian woman?

Anorexic.

The Jewish woman and the black man had a little boy. One day, the boy came home from school obviously distressed. "What's wrong?" his mother asked.

"I've gotta know if I'm more Jewish or more black," the boy said.

"That's a tough one, son," the mother said. "Why don't you ask your father."

The little boy waited until Dad came home from work. When he popped the question, his father demanded to be told why he wanted to know. "You see, Freddy down the street has a bike to sell. I don't know whether to bargain him down or just wait until dark and steal it."

———————

Did you hear about the Polack who died of shit in his veins?

He'd been trying to shoot crap.

Why did the Polack bring a box of condoms to school?

The teacher said they were going to study the Trojan War.

Why do Japanese women hate oral sex?

When Japanese men smell raw fish, they can't help biting.

How can you tell when a black woman needs to douche?

When the cockroaches start dying.

Two black chicks were sitting on the stoop when one noticed the other scratching at her crotch. She thought for a moment, then said, "Girl, why you be itching? You got the crabs?"

"I can't get no crabs."

"What you mean?"

"Leroy done told me I's never gonno get no crabs, 'long as he sticks his Black Flag in me twice a night."

———————————

Why don't Puerto Rican dogs do any tricks?

To teach tricks, you have to be smarter than the dog.

———————————

What do you call a teenage black kid who won't take a free vial of crack?

Dead.

Why did the hooker turn away the Indian john?

Her doctor told her not to eat red meat.

_____

What does it mean to "renig?"

To change shifts at a car wash.

_____

What's Farm Aid?

One redneck holds down a pig so another red-neck can fuck it.

Did you hear about the Polack who died cooking dinner?

He put his nose in the microwave.

Why are black kids so jealous of their Cabbage Patch Dolls?

Cabbage Patch Dolls have birth certificates.

Chapter Two:

Gross News Jokes

What's the only good thing to come out of the Branch Davidian fire in Waco?

David Koresh finally stopped smoking.

Did you hear that the Branch Davidians changed their name?

They're now the Ignited Church of Christ.

Did you hear about the new Branch Davidian charcoal?

Your fire will be simply divine.

_____

What did Henry VII say to his lawyer?

"Screw the divorce. I've got a better idea."

_____

Did you hear that Bill Clinton has created a new cabinet post devoted to women's affairs?

It's called the Secretary of the Inferior.

Why was being a Branch Davidian such a lousy job?

No matter what a person did, he ended up being fired.

What does Jerry Falwell eat when he's constipated?

Moral fiber.

God was sitting on his throne in heaven one day when George Bush died and appeared in front of him. God said, "Sir, what did you accomplish during your life?"

Bush said, "I was President of the United States."

God said, "Then you may take the seat at my left hand."

Later, Bill Clinton died and appeared in heaven. God asked him, "Sir, what did you accomplish during your life?"

Clinton said, "I was President of the United States."

So God said, "You may sit at my right hand."

Sometime after that, Hillary Clinton died. She appeared in heaven, took a quick look, and said to God, "Hey, what are you doing in my chair?"

Why did all the necrophiliacs rush to Waco?

They heard about some really *hot* pieces of ass.

Did you hear about the financial problems at the Children's Television Workshop?

They had to shoot a kiddie porn movie called, *Sesame Street Presents: Swallow That Bird*.

What do the airlines do with used vomit bags?

Donate them to Bosnia Relief and take a tax write-off.

What goes "hop, skip, jump, boom?"

Bosnian children playing in a mine field.

How do Bosnian soldiers keep their bayonets sharp?

They keep a dead baby on the tip.

———————————

How do they take the census in Bosnia?

They add up the number of arms and legs and divide by 2.

Chapter Three:

Gross Animal Jokes

What's the definition of a nervous animal?

A race horse with a Greek jockey.

_____

What's an Australian's idea of romantic music?

A tape of sheep bleating.

Two sharks were swimming in the ocean when one turned to the other and said, "Wow, my ass really burns."

The other one said, "See, I told you not to eat that Mexican."

———————

Two dogs were walking down the street when they came to a parking meter. One turned to the other and said, "How do you like that?"

"How do I like what?"

The dog pointed his paw at the meter and said, "That, the pay toilet."

———————

The country girl walked into the doctor's office and said, "I'm ashamed to admit it. But last week I got so horny I put some birdseed in my cunt and got my canary to peck it out. Now my cunt's all itchy and sore."

The doctor inspected her and said, "I'm afraid I've got some bad news. You've got twerpies."

"Is that bad?" she asked.

"Bad! It's untweetable!"

Of all the world's men, who has the most girl-friends?

Scotsmen. About two hundred in every flock.

———————————

Why didn't the farm boy want to bring his girl friend to the high school dance?

She was Bossie.

———————————

What's the first thing to remember about fucking a female elephant?

Never let her get on top.

Three bulls were standing in the pasture grousing about the expected arrival of a fourth bull. They were posturing about the damage they were going to inflict on the new rival when a truck pulled up, and out stepped the biggest, blackest, strongest, meanest looking bull anyone had ever seen.

The first bull, who had 20 cows, turned to his friends and said, "Well, 20 cows is a tiring job. I guess I could use a little help."

The second bull said, "Ten cows sometimes does me in. I wouldn't mind sharing a bit."

The third bull, who had only five cows, was raging and snorting like he was spoiling for a fight. The first bull said, "I can't believe that you're willing to get pummelled for a measly five cows."

"I'm not worried about that," the third one replied. "I just want him to know I'm a *bull*."

Why aren't Volkswagens allowed in Africa?

Because an elephant will screw anything with a trunk in front of it.

_____

How much did the whorehouse charge the elephant?

$35 for the lay and $350 for the condom.

_____

What's pink, wet, smells like tuna, and weighs 200 pounds?

An elephant's cunt.

What's so bad about being captured by a gross elephant?

He makes you pick his nose.

———————

How bad was last summer's drought down South?

Two trees were destroyed fighting over a dog.

———————

What do you call it when you dream about fucking large animals?

An elephantasy.

———————

What do elephants use for tampons?

Sheep.

Why do elephants have trunks?

Because sheep don't have strings.

What happens to female elephants who use sheep as tampons?

They come down with Toxic Flock Syndrome.

Why are an elephant's toes yellow?

He's too big to raise his leg to pee.

Who's two feet tall and has an eight-foot dick?

A guy who's been blown by an elephant.

What are the most sexually frustrated animals in the world?

Camels. Most of them only get one hump.

A puppy was sleeping on the railroad tracks when a train suddenly appeared. The groggy little dog tried to scramble out of the way, but the train ran over his tail, cutting off a small piece. The puppy climbed back up the bank to the tracks to find the missing piece. He reached the top just as a train barrelled down from the other direction and cut off his head.

Moral: Don't lose your head over a little piece of tail.

Who circumcises whales?

Fore-skin divers.

What do you call a rabbit with crabs?

Bugs Bunny.

———————————

How can you tell an elephant has been screwing your wife?

When her cunt's wider than her hips.

———————————

What should you do when you pass an elephant?

Unclog the toilet.

———————————

What do female rabbits like to lick?

Hare balls.

Chapter Four:

Gross Homosexual Jokes

What do you call it when a bunch of fags get together to talk about their sex lives?

An organ recital.

A lesbian and a gay rights activist were passengers in a small plane flying to a demonstration when the plane crash-landed in the water. The pilot was killed, but the two managed to swim to a deserted island.

A week later, they were both found dead. At a press conference, a reporter asked, "Did they die of their injuries or starvation?"

The spokesperson said, "No. They survived the crash intact and the island had plenty of food and water."

"Then how did they die?"

"Apparently," the spokesperson said, "they strangled each other in an argument over who would do what to whom."

What's the definition of a considerate gay lover?

A guy who doesn't make you give him a blow-job after he buttfucks you.

How can you tell if a dyke is really tough?

She uses a brick for a tampon.

How can you tell if a female tennis player is gay?

She douches in Gatorade.

_____

Why do so many faggots suffer from depression?

It's tough enough to be rejected by women.

_____

What do you call a lesbian trucker?

A van dyke.

_____

Why is gay sex like kindergarten?

If you want to stay out of trouble, sit down and keep your mouth shut.

The faggot walked into his apartment one day and said to his lover, "Bruce, I've got some bad news for you. I've got AIDS."

Bruce exploded, "I don't believe it. We're so careful. How did you get AIDS?"

"I got it from a toilet seat," the first fag said.

"You can't get AIDS from a toilet seat," Bruce said.

"You can if you sit down before the last guy gets up!"

———————

Why are the best commandoes gay?

They're experts on attacking from the rear.

———————

What was the dying transvestite's last request?

He wanted to be buried a broad.

The faggot arrived home early from work one day to find his roommate Bruce getting screwed in the ass. He exclaimed, "That's it. I'm leaving. I simply can't go through this again."

The roommate said, "Chet, darling, you know we agreed that we could see other men."

"I know," Chet said. "But it turns out I just can't stand the idea of someone else opening my male."

———————

Why is gay sex like flipping a coin?

You can choose head or tail.

———————

How can you tell a transvestite bar?

It always has a dress code.

Two faggots were shouting insults at each other, and one was about to start pulling the other's hair when a cop came up and said, "Hey, knock it off."

They stopped for a moment, and the cop asked, "What's this about?"

"Just an argument, officer," one said.

Then the cop turned around and saw a handsome young stud standing against the wall, his bulging member pushing against his tight shorts. "And what's that?" he asked.

One of the faggots replied, "That's the bone of contention."

———————

Did you hear about the new brand of lesbian shoes?

They're manufactured with extra-long tongues.

What's anal sex?

The man in the moon.

_____

What's a gay's idea of a Big Mac?

A Whopper that cums on his buns.

_____

What's an orthodox fag?

A guy who only eats kosher weinies.

_____

Why did the gay guy call his boyfriend "Lolly-pop?"

He's hard for the first few licks, melts in his mouth, and leaves his face sticky afterwards.

Why is a guy with AIDS so dull?

If you give him an opening, he'll bore you to death.

———————————

Why is AIDS like a cold?

You're less likely to catch it if you're wearing rubbers.

———————————

How can you tell if an Indian is gay?

All his scalps have handles.

———————————

Did you hear that they have a new form of death by injection in Texas?

A fag with AIDS fucks you in the ass.

Why aren't there many gay necrophiliacs anymore?

After the AIDS epidemic, most have died of exhaustion.

_____

What's one benefit of allowing gays in the military?

We'll be the world's best in close order drilling.

_____

What's the downside of gays in the military?

Our Army will be a collection of the world's biggest assholes.

Why do so many fags want to join the Army when it's so physically grueling?

They've decided the ends justify the means.

———————

How can you tell if a platoon has gay soldiers?

They're doing push-ups in pairs.

———————

How are they planning to make gays feel more welcome in the Army?

They're changing the name of Fort Benning to Fort Bruce.

How can you tell a basic training company has a lot of lesbians?

All the M-16 barrels smell like tuna.

———————

How would you describe today's soldiers?

Comrades-in-arms.

Chapter Five:

A Gross Assortment

Why shouldn't a blind man go bungee jumping?

It'd scare the shit out of his dog.

The gorgeous young model wanted to file for divorce, and the moment she walked into the office of her handsome divorce attorney the air was filled with electricity. After a few moments of conversation, the heat built up to the point where the lawyer locked his door, then passionately embraced her. Clothes were everywhere as they feverishly coupled once, then a second time.

Exhausted, they dressed. The lawyer resumed asking questions about the case, making page after page of notes. Finally, he said, "I guess that's all for now. I'll file the papers first thing next week."

She smiled. "Thanks a lot. I never knew legal affairs could be so much fun. What about our getting together for a repeat this weekend?"

The lawyer's mouth opened in shock. "You mean, on my own time?"

The fourth grade teacher was giving a vocabulary lesson. She told the class, "I want you to give me a three-syllable word that describes something in this room, then use it in a sentence."

Little Amy raised her hand and said, "Violet. Teacher's dress is violet."

"Very good," the teacher said, then she pointed to another girl.

"Complexion," Jessica said. "Our teacher has a lovely complexion."

The teacher beamed. "That's wonderful. Anyone else?"

A boy in the back of his room raised his hand. When he was recognized, he said, "Urinate."

The teacher's face wrinkled in disgust. "Brad, that's awful."

"No, it isn't," Brad said. "Urinate. But if your ass was bigger, you'd be a ten."

A blind man walked into a store and started knocking things off the shelf with his cane. The manager hurried up and said, "Sir, can I help you?"

"No thanks," the blind man replied. "I'm just looking."

———————

The mother of the high school senior walked into her son's bedroom one day to see him kneeling in front of his best friend while sucking his cock. She screamed, "What are you doing?"

The boy said, "It was Dad's idea."

The mother said, "Your father would never tell you to do this!"

"Yes, he did," the boy said. "I told him I couldn't get my mind off girls." He pointed to a shaker sitting on the floor, then added, "He told me I wouldn't get so horny if I had some salt peter."

The naughty little boy came up to a little girl and said, "Jackie, can I lift up your dress and put my finger in your belly button?"

She said, "Go ahead."

"You sure?"

"I'm sure."

He moved forward. A moment later, she said, "Hey, that's not my belly button."

"That's okay," the boy said, panting. "That's not my finger."

———————

The little boy baby and the little girl baby were sleeping in separate cribs when the little girl baby suddenly woke up and started shouting, "Rape, rape, rape!"

The little boy baby woke up, looked over at her for a second, then said, "Aw, shut up! You're just sleeping on your pacifier."

The foursome was walking down the fairway when one guy said to Bob, "You look distracted today. Is there anything wrong?"

Bob said, "Well, I'm going in tomorrow for an operation."

"What kind?"

Bob hesitated for a moment, then he said, "Look, you guys are my best friends. I guess I owe you an explanation. You've probably noticed I never shower with you or change in the locker room. That's because I was born a hermaphrodite—a person with both male and female genitalia. Tomorrow I'm going in to have my vagina sewn up."

"Are you crazy?" one of his friends said. "Have them cut off your balls. Then you can hit from the red tees."

About twenty minutes after teeing off, the woman comes back into the clubhouse grimacing in pain. The club pro asked, "What happened?"

She gasped, "I was stung by a bee."

"Where?"

She said, "Between the first and second holes."

"Hmmm," the pro said, "your stance was probably too wide."

How does an old man keep his youth?

By giving her lots of money.

Why don't old women have any respect for old men?

They're just putty in their hands.

The foursome was walking down the fairway when they noticed a group of eight-year-old boys playing in the rough. As they grew closer, they realized that the boys were all shouting things like, "Fuck you. God damn, son of a bitch. Jesus fucking Christ. Shit on a stick."

One man walked over and said to the boys, "What's wrong with you boys? You shouldn't be using language like that."

One boy said, "Well, we're too young to actually play golf. We're just practicing for when we grow up."

_____

During a recess period, two dogs started fucking in the schoolyard. Embarrassed, the teacher ordered one of the older boys to break them up. He couldn't do it, and neither could three other boys who tried.

Finally, little Nicky, who was in the third grade, stepped up and said, "I can do it." The older boys laughed, but the teacher told him he could try. Nicky walked over to the two animals and stuck his finger up the ass of the male dog. Immediately, the dog pulled out and ran away.

"How did you learn to do that?" the teacher asked.

Nicky replied, "That there was old Ben. He can dish it out, but he can't take it."

74

What do you get when you cross a Cabbage Patch Doll with the Pillsbury dough boy?

A rich bitch with a yeast infection.

When should you suspect your kid has a drug problem?

When his pet rock is from Bolivia.

What do you call it when your 13-year-old daughter leaves home and gets pregnant?

Runaway inflation.

A man was sitting at the breakfast table one morning when his eight-year-old son came up to him and said, "Daddy, I've decided I want to be just like you."

Flattered, his father said, "Son, I'm glad you want to be a lawyer."

"That isn't what I mean," the boy replied. "I mean I want to fuck Mommy."

———————

Mel the lawyer got a call late one night from one of his clients. Half an hour later, he was down at the city jail, where his client Fred was sobbing in a cell.

"Why are you here?" Mel asked.

"It's my wife," sobbed Fred. "She's a lousy mother."

"You were arrested because your wife's a lousy mother?"

"Yeah," Fred replied "Last night we had one of our big fights. Finally, I threw the baby at her. And that bitch, she's such a lousy mother that she ducked."

A guy was walking down the street behind a blind man. Suddenly, the blind man's seeing eye dog stopped, lifted his leg, and pissed all over his master's leg. Then, to the amazement of the onlooker, the blind man reached into his pocket and gave the dog a biscuit.

The guy who'd been watching caught up with the blind man at the next corner. He touched him on the arm and said, "Excuse me, but I gotta know. Why did you give your dog a treat after he'd pissed on your leg."

"I wasn't rewarding him," the blind man growled. "I wanted to find out where his head was so I could kick him in the ass."

———————

Did you hear about the queer deaf mute?

Neither did he.

A few weeks after his parents' divorce, little Joey passed by his mother's bedroom. The door was ajar, and when he peeked in, he saw his mother lying naked on the bed, rubbing herself all over as she moaned, "I need a man. I need a man."

The scene was repeated several times over the next month. Finally, one night, Joey got up to use the bathroom. As he passed his mother's room, he saw a guy on top of her, pumping away.

Immediately, Joey turned around and ran back to his room. He stripped off his clothes and jumped on the bed. Then he started rubbing himself all over and moaned, "I need a bike. I need a bike. . . ."

A little boy, the oldest of six kids, was sitting in the kitchen with his parents when he asked "Dad, why can't trains have little trains like people have little people?"

Immediately, the mother retorted, "Because unlike your father, trains pull out on time."

What did the man say to the one-legged hitch-hiker?

"Hop in."

───────────────

What kind of music do vampires love?

Ragtime.

───────────────

To a vampire, why are women like a hockey game?

For both, there's far too long a time between periods.

───────────────

Why do most vampires live in the South?

They love rednecks.

Why did the cannibal rush over to the cafeteria?

He heard children were half price.

———————

Fred was taking his son Joey to the ballgame for the first time, and he wanted to make sure the kid had a good time. Before they went to their seats, Fred stopped at the refreshment stand and bought the kid two hot dogs with mustard and sauerkraut, french fries, and a large Coke.

In the first inning, Joey turned to his dad and started to say, "Daddy, I want. . . ."

Fred interrupted, "I know, you want popcorn." He motioned the vender over and bought a large bag.

The next inning, Joey said, "Daddy, I want. . . ."

Fred stopped him again and bought cotton candy.

The third inning, Joey said, "Daddy, I really want. . . ."

"It's ice cream," Fred said. He bought a big cup.

The next inning, Joey turned to Fred and vomited noisily into his lap.

"What in the hell did you do that for?" the Father demanded.

Joey replied, "Since the first inning, I've been trying to tell you I want to throw up."

A Scotsman was washed overboard in the midst of a terrible storm. Hours later, he struggled out of the ocean onto a remote African shore, only to be captured by cannibals.

The cannibals put him in a cage and carried him back to their village. He expected to be put into a pot, but instead, he was given food and water. The next evening, however, the cannibals came by, stuck a spear in his arm, drained off some blood, and went away.

The procedure was the same for a week. Finally, the Scotsman saw the cannibals coming again and he howled, "Ye bastard savages. Put me in a pot and eat me if you will. But you're not sticking me for drinks again."

———————

Why did the cannibals capture the Olympic team?

They love fast food.

Why did the cannibal call the dating service?

Take-out food.

_____

Why don't cannibals eat drug addicts?

Junk food isn't good for them.

_____

How can you tell a cannibal's a fussy eater?

He'll eat arms, but he spits out the pits.

_____

What's a bat cave?

A lady vampire's cunt.

What does a vampire call it when his girlfriend gets her period?

Happy hour.

_____

What do cannibals call paraplegics?

Meals on wheels.

_____

Did you hear about the cannibal who broke into the grammar school?

Two days later, he passed the second grade.

Why did the vampire give his girlfriend a blood test?

To see if she was his type.

_____

The mother came out into the backyard. Her little eight-year-old daughter was standing a couple inches from the boy next door. As she approached, she was surprised to see Sally was huffing and puffing in the boy's face.

"What are you doing?" she asked.

Sally replied, "We're playing hospital, and I'm a nurse, just like my big sister Jane."

"What are you doing to Timmy?"

"Just what I heard Jane talk about on the phone last night. He's a doctor, and I'm blowing him."

Chapter Six:

Gross Medical Jokes

Why did the dentist have the glass removed from his office windows?

He wanted to advertise himself as "paneless."

_____

Did you hear about the Tibetan monk who wouldn't take Novocaine when he had his tooth filled?

He wanted to transcend dental meditation.

A guy walked into a dentist office and complained, "Doc, I lost all of my teeth last night."

The dentist said, "How could you lose every single one of your teeth in one night?"

The guy said, "I don't know. I went to sleep with my head under the pillow and next thing I knew, my teeth were gone and my mouth was full of quarters."

———————

The surgeon went on a deer hunting weekend. When he walked into the hospital on Monday morning, his nurse asked, "How did it go?"

The sawbones grimaced. "I didn't kill a thing."

The nurse said, "That's too bad. You'd have been better off staying here."

The patient had had a throat operation, and the only way he could get nutrition was through his ass. One morning the nurse walked into his room. The patient handed her a note that read, "Could I please have an extra enema bag this noon?"

"Why?" she asked.

He grabbed a pad and wrote, "I'd like to invite someone to lunch."

———————

The man was on the phone with the hospital arranging his admission. At the end of the conversation, the hospital clerk said, "One last reminder. When you come, we want to emphasize 'TLC.'"

"You mean, 'tender, loving care?' " the future patient asked.

"No," the clerk replied. "I mean, 'Take lotsa cash.' "

The doctor and his wife got into an awful argument about their sex life. He finally shouted, "The only real problem we have is that you're a god-awful fuck!" Then he stormed out of the house.

A couple hours later, the doctor began to feel guilty. He stopped for a dozen roses, then tiptoed into his bedroom. To his surprise, his wife was screwing another man.

"Just what in the hell do you think you're doing?" he demanded.

His wife looked at him calmly and said, "I'm doing what you always recommend—I'm getting a second opinion."

———————

What was so unusual about the hypochondriac's will?

He wanted to be buried next to a doctor.

What's another name for a gynecologist?

A privates investigator.

———————————

Did you hear about the obstetrician who worked his way through medical school in the post office?

It now takes him a week to deliver a baby.

———————————

The naive young woman had just finished her gynecological exam when the doctor asked if she had any questions. She said timidly, "Well, I do have one, though it may be silly. Is . . . is it possible to become pregnant through anal sex?"

The doctor said, "That's not a silly question at all. Where do you think lawyers come from?"

The woman was sitting in the psychiatrist's office when she confessed, "Doctor, I'm a nymphomaniac. You've got to help me."

"I would like to," the shrink said, "but I could concentrate better if you'd stop licking my dick."

_____

When do patients understand why psychiatrists are called "shrinks?"

When they take a look at their bank statements.

_____

What do gynecologists have for breakfast?

A bagel with a smear.

Did you hear about the lazy dentist?

He swept his patients' tartar under their gums.

The doctor came into the waiting room and said to the man, "I'm sorry to give you some bad news. Your wife is at death's door."

The man said, "Doctor, promise me one thing—you'll do everything you can to pull her through."

A man ran into the emergency room, grabbed a guy in a white coat, and said, "Doctor, quick! Do you know a cure for the worst case of hiccups in history?"

The doctor turned and kneed the man in the groin. He gasped, taking in a huge gulp of air as he doubled over. "There," the doctor said, "I bet you don't have the hiccups anymore."

"No," the man wheezed, "but my wife out in the car does."

How can you tell a woman is a practical nurse?

She marries a rich doctor.

―――――――

A guy walked into the doctor's office and said, "Doc, I've been sleepwalking every night and I'm exhausted. How can I stop?"

"Simple," the doctor said. "Spread thumbtacks on the floor."

―――――――

A hysterical woman called the doctor's office and said, "You've got to help me! My baby just fell down a well."

"Calm down, the doctor said. "All you have to do is go out and get a copy of Dr. Spock's book."

"Dr. Spock's book?" she shouted. "How in the world could that possibly help?"

The doctor replied, "It will tell you how to raise a baby."

The rather heavy-set woman had her feet up in the stirrups at the gynecologist's office when she said, "Doc, I've got the feeling I'm loosing my sex appeal. What can I do?"

He said, "Above all, I'd recommend that you diet."

"Really?" she said. "What color?"

Chapter Seven:

Gross No Arms
No Legs Jokes

What do you call a guy with no arms and no legs who's been dropped into a swimming pool?

Bob.

_____

What do you call a guy with no arms and no legs who's thrown across the surface of a pond?

Skip.

What do you call a guy with no arms and no legs who's been nailed to the wall?

Art.

———————

What do you call a guy with no arms and no legs who's helping to change a tire?

Jack.

———————

What do you call a guy with no arms and no legs who has no head and no torso?

Dick.

———————

What do you call a guy with no arms and no legs who's been tossed into an Irish fireplace?

Pete.

What do you call a guy with no arms and no legs who always get shit on?

John.

What do you call a guy with no arms and no legs who has pictures nailed to him?

Wally.

What do you call a guy with no arms and no legs who arrives in your mailbox once a month?

Bill.

What do you call a guy with no arms and no legs who's in a pot with a bunch of vegetables?

Stu.

What do you call a guy with no arms and no legs who's lying in front of your door?

Matt.

_____

What do you call a guy with no arms and no legs who's covered with mustard?

Frank.

_____

What do you call a guy with no arms and no legs who's covered with sauerkraut and Russian dressing?

Reuben.

_____

What do you call a guy with no arms and no legs who smashes up several wheelchairs?

Rex.

What do you call a guy with no arms and no legs who's upside down in the end zone?

Spike.

––––––––––––––––

What do you call a guy with no arms and no legs who's been attacked by lions?

Claude.

––––––––––––––––

What do you call a guy with no arms and no legs who tastes good?

Winston.

––––––––––––––––

What do you call a woman with no arms and no legs who's floating upside down in a pool?

Fannie.

What do you call a woman with no arms and no legs who's caught on a fence?

Barb.

_____

What do you call a woman with no arms and no legs who's on a bun?

Patti.

_____

What do you call a woman with no arms and no legs on toast?

Marge.

_____

What do you call a woman with no arms and no legs hanging in a steeple?

Belle.

What do you call a woman with no arms and no legs with a weak bladder?

Pia.

_____

What do you call a woman with no arms and no legs who's very popular with the boys?

Heddie.

_____

What do you call a woman with no arms and no legs who has no head and no torso?

Muffie.

_____

What do you call a woman with no arms and no legs whose parachute didn't open?

Dot.

What do you call a woman with no arms and no legs who's been washed ashore?

Sandi.

_____

What do you call a woman with no arms and no legs who's surrounded by hungry truckers?

Dinah.

_____

What do you call a woman with no arms and no legs who takes people to court?

Sue.

_____

What do you call a woman with no arms and no legs who rolls around on wheels?

Dolly.

What do you call a woman with no arms and no legs who's potted?

Fern.

What do you call a woman with no arms and no legs who's a little under par?

Birdie.

What do you call a woman with no arms and no legs who's been stared at by gypsies?

Crystal.

What do you call a woman with no arms and no legs who's been captured by cannibals?

Candy.

_____

What do you call a woman with no arms and one leg?

Peg.

Chapter Eight:

Gross Religious Jokes

The young man entered the monastery, and on the first day he was given all the rules. The monk with whom he was to share a small room said, "The only time we are normally permitted to speak is at mealtimes. Silence is particularly important at night, which we devote to meditation and prayer."

The monks returned to their rooms at night. The young man found the absolute silence to be very peaceful. He was absorbed in prayer when, suddenly, a loud scream echoed through the halls. The young man jumped and before he could think shouted, "Someone's in trouble. We've got to help!"

The monk said, "Sit down and be quiet. It's nothing. Brother Malcom just forgot the Abbott has piles."

One day two nuns were walking in the park when one said, "Let's stop and pray."

"All right," her friend said. Then she proceeded to pull down her panties, get down on all fours, and pulled her habit up over her head so her ass was exposed.

The other nun was shocked. "Sister Mary-Marie! What do you think you're doing?"

"Be quiet and watch," Sister Mary-Marie said.

Sure enough, in a couple minutes, some guy came along and answered her prayer.

———————

A young boy snuck into the church, sat down in a pew, and began jerking off. A few minutes later, a nun came in, saw what he was doing, and shouted, "Stop that. That's a mortal sin."

"No, it's not," the boy said calmly. "Remember, the Lord helps those that help themselves."

Father Flynn and Rabbi Dobkin were talking one night when the priest said, "Rabbi Dobkin, temptation is always with us as we honor the Lord. If you don't mind a personal question, have you ever sinned by eating pork?"

The Rabbi said, "I have. I was about to order in a diner one day when I became obsessed with the idea of ordering a BLT. I fought against the urge, but eventually I gave in. I was just a young man, but I felt guilty for years." He paused, then asked, "So, Father, what about you? It's a sin for you to have sex, isn't it?"

Father Flynn said, "Yes, it is. But tell me: isn't eating pussy a lot more fun than eating bacon?"

A Jew, a Catholic, and a Mormon were bragging about their families. The Jew said, "I've got five strong, healthy boys. That's enough for an entire basketball team."

"You think that's a lot," said the Catholic. "Well, I've got eight kids and my wife's got another bun in the oven. When that one's born, I'll have my own baseball team."

The Mormon was unimpressed. "You want to talk about family? I've got seventeen wives. One more and I've got my own golf course!"

What is an artificial inseminary?

A place where nuns go to get pregnant.

What's a black cherry?

A Negro nun.

What's cherry pop?

What happens when you rape a nun.

What're cherry turnovers?

Nuns leaving the convent.

What's cherry pie?

Eating a nun.

What's cherry jam?

Three guys trying to fuck the same nun.

What's cherries jubilee?

Fourteen nuns in a hot tub.

_____

What are cherry pits?

The hair under a nun's arms.

_____

What's a cherry sucker?

A nun giving you a blowjob.

_____

What's cherry juice?

A nun giving you a golden shower.

What would you say about a nun who wiped her ass with her clothes?

I'd say she had a filthy habit.

———————

Why is space a vacuum?

Because God sucks.

———————

Why do Catholic priests believe in the Ten Commandments?

Because there's no commandment against blowing altar boys.

Did you hear about the progressive Catholic school that started sex education?

They take kids to the zoo to watch monkeys fuck.

———————

Why did the young girl leave the convent?

She learned "nun" really meant "none."

———————

A priest and a rabbi decided to buy a car together, since they couldn't afford new cars on their own. They went down to the local dealership and got a good deal on a new Ford LTD. The day they signed the papers, they made a deal among themselves that the vehicle wouldn't be either Catholic or Jewish.

That night, however, the priest climbed out of bed, went out to the garage, and sprinkled holy water under the hood—totally unaware that the rabbi had heard him. The next night, the rabbi sneaked out to the garage, got out a hacksaw, and took four inches off the tailpipe.

An elderly Jew was rushed to a Catholic hospital for an emergency operation. A nun asked him who would be responsible for the bill. The old man said, "I've only got one relative, a sister. But she's an old maid who converted to Catholicism and became a nun."

Indignantly, the nun retorted, "We nuns are not old maids—we're married to Jesus Christ."

"In that case," the Jew said, "send the bill to my brother-in-law."

Why couldn't Jesus work for the Red Cross?

It's a non-*prophet* business.

How do priests get little kids to suck their pricks?

By telling them they're cream-filled.

How do you know your son's been abused by a priest?

When his asshole opens wider than his mouth.

―――――――――

How do you know your son's been molested by a priest?

When he comes home from church, it takes you an hour every night to comb the cum out of his hair.

―――――――――

What's another way you know your son's been molested?

When he kneels down for communion, he unzips the priest's fly.

How can you tell your son's being molested?

He won't eat a hot dog unless it's got hair around it.

———————————

Why are so many Catholic parishes launching fund drives?

The price of Vaseline is rising.

———————————

Why do Catholic priests wear black?

It's harder to see where the shit stains on their dicks rub off.

Chapter Nine:

Gross Sex Jokes

The loser was sitting at the bar, quietly sobbing into his beer. Another guy came up and asked, "What's the problem?"

The loser said, "I just found out that sperm banks pay $20 for a donation."

"So why are you crying?"

"I've let a fortune slip through my fingers!" the loser wailed.

Why is it better for a woman to be beautiful instead of smart?

Nobody puts a hand up a dress looking for a library card.

Why is sex with your wife like a 7-Eleven?

There's not much variety, but at 2 a.m., it's always there.

What's another name for high school sex education?

Prom night.

A guy was walking down the street when a panhandler grabbed his arm and said, "Hey, mac. Help me out. I need $20 to get laid."

The man tried to pull away.

"Please," the bum said. "I haven't had sex in a month."

The guy, angry, said, "You've got a lot of nerve! If you want to get laid, you should have gotten married."

The bum was shocked. "Then I'd have to beg for sex *every* night!"

———————————

The owner of a nudist colony looked up to see a fully clothed man wandering among the guests. He went over to the guy and asked, "May I help you?"

"No, thanks," the man said. "I'm just browsing."

———————————

Why did the hooker go back to school to study psychology?

She decided she'd rather blow men's minds.

The drunk staggered up to the beat cop and stammered, "Officer, you gotta help me."

"What's wrong?" the cop asked.

The drunk said, "My car's been stolen." He stuck out his index finger and said, "See this. I had my key ring around it just a minute ago."

The policeman grimaced in disgust. "How do you expect me to believe you have a car. You haven't shaved in a week, you stink, and your clothes are filthy. And besides, your fly is down and your dick is sticking out."

"Oh, my god!" the drunk exclaimed. "Somebody stole my girl friend!"

———————

Did you hear about the group that wants to eliminate fellatio?

They call themselves the "gum control lobby."

Did you hear about the massage parlor worker who was an avid New York baseball fan?

On the job, she yanked roots, and in her spare time she. . . .

———————

Why don't hookers eat much junk food?

Their work is so filling.

———————

The husband had been trying to persuade his wife to give him a blowjob, but she resisted. Finally, he took out his prick and said, "Look. You always tell me it makes you feel better when I stick this in you. Right?"

"That's right," the wife replied.

"Well," the husband said. "I just want you to have a taste of your own medicine."

What's a prime example of an "enigma?"

The fact that graffiti is always worse in the men's room when women have both hands free.

The husband was in back, pumping away doggie-style when his wife turned around and yelled, "Hey, why do we always have to do it this way? You got something against my face?"

The husband shrugged, "Your ass, your face—either way, it's just a hole to stick my dick in."

The husband arrived home with a dozen roses and handed them to his wife. Without a word, she took his hand and led him to the bedroom. She took off all of her clothes, lay down on the bed with her legs spread, and said, "This is for the roses."

"They'd fit," he said, "and you probably wouldn't feel the thorns."

Why do female sky divers wear tampons?

So they don't whistle on the way down.

_____

Why did God give women two holes so close to each other?

In case men miss.

_____

How can you tell if a guy is a loser?

The mirror over his bed reads, "Objects are larger than they appear to be."

How do we know men invented maps?

Who else would make one inch equal a hundred miles?

———————————

Why did God create woman?

After he created man, he said, "I think I can do a whole lot better."

———————————

As usual, she was jumping out of her skin, so she went to see a doctor who specialized in women's health. After a thorough examination he called her into his office and said, "I have some good news and some bad news for you."

"What's the good news?" she asked.

"The good news is you don't have PMS. The bad news is you're just a bitch."

The cruise ship sank. Three survivors, a married couple and a cabin boy, made it to a small deserted island. There was very little privacy, and the handsome young cabin boy grew hornier and hornier as he watched the couple have sex. He was even more frustrated because the looks the woman gave him told him she was interested, too.

One day, the cabin boy climbed up the 50-foot palm tree to look for passing ships. Suddenly, he called down, "Hey, from up here, it looks like you're fucking."

The husband called back, "We're just sitting here." Then he turned to his wife and said, "He must be going stir crazy."

Late that afternoon, it was the husband's turn to climb the tree to look for ships. When he got to the top, he suddenly yelled, "Hey, you're right. It does look like fucking down there!"

The Wall Street wheeler and dealer came home unexpectedly one afternoon and found his wife romping in bed with a naked young man. His face reddened, and he shouted, "What's the meaning of this?"

"It's simple," his wife replied. "I've gone public."

————————

The man was walking down the street when a young woman in hot pants and a halter top came up and said, "Please donate," and held up a cup that read "Keep Prostitutes Off the Street."

The man said, "How much are you looking for?"

She winked at him and said, "It depends on how long you want to keep me off the street."

Once again, the wife complained about sleeping on the wet spot. Finally, her husband said, "Shut up. It's your fault."

"How can it be my fault?" she asked.

He said, "If you'd swallow it, there wouldn't *be* a wet spot."

———————

Why are masturbators so patriotic?

When they yank their doodle, they feel dandy.

———————

How can you tell if a guy is a real loser?

You tell him you need a lubricant in bed, and he pulls out a can of Crisco.

How can you tell if your date's a real loser?

When he turns around to close the door, you can read what brand of underwear he's wearing.

———————

How do you know a guy's a loser?

He's the one trying to hit on women at the V.D. clinic.

———————

What's the definition of a great blind date?

You ask her to dance and she takes off her clothes and climbs up on a table.

How do they play strip poker in a nudist colony?

With a pair of tweezers.

The couple were all over each other in a dark booth. Then the waitress came over and said, "I better cut your husband off. He just slid under the table."

The woman said, "You're wrong. My husband just walked in the door."

What's a humdinger?

A girl who hums every time she sees a dinger.

The couple had been back from their honeymoon a couple of weeks and the fire was beginning to wane. One day the guy came home from work and said, "Honey, we're going to make love a new way tonight."

"Great," his bride said. "What's that?"

"Well," the guy said, "we're going to take off all of our clothes and lie back to back."

She looked puzzled. "How can that be any fun?"

He replied, "Because I've invited another couple."

The husband and wife had not been able to conceive after almost two years of trying, so the doctor called her in and said, "Perhaps your husband's sperm count is low. I think you ought to consider artificial insemination."

"What's that?" she asked.

"Well," he said, pulling out a test tube, "we take sperm like this from a donor and we insert it where your husband shoots his sperm."

"That's fine with me," the wife said. Then she grabbed the test tube and drank it.

———————————

What's a sardine?

A little fish that smells like your finger.

What goes "Ha, ha, ha, ha, ha, ha, thump, thump?"

A guy laughing his balls off.

A guy walked into the rest room of the bar just in time to see his friend Ed kissing the cunt of a scuzzy old whore. In disgust, he immediately walked out the door. When his friend came out, he said, "Ed, why in heaven's name would you kiss her raunchy old snatch?"

"To cure my chapped lips," Ed replied.

"How does kissing that cunt cure chapped lips?"

"Well," Ed said, "now, I'm sure I won't lick them."

A guy was on the phone with a salesman. Finally, the salesman said, "I'll tell you what I'll do. I'll give it to you for $600 minus 6% for cash."

The guy tried to do the calculation in his head for a minute. Then he put his hand over the phone, turned to his wife, and said, "Honey, if you were offered $600 minus 6%, how much would you take off?"

"Everything but my earrings," she replied.

———————

Did you hear about the guy with the incredibly long tongue?

When he stuck it out for the doctor, the nurse fainted.

What's love?

The delusion that one woman is different from another.

_____

Did you hear about the farsighted golfer?

He drove his caddies nuts.

One guy ran into a friend at the tennis club and asked, "Fred, how come Bob isn't your partner in the doubles tournament this year?"

Fred said, "Let me put it this way. Would you be partners with a guy who borrowed money he didn't return, always yelled at you for every mistake, and tried to screw both your wife and your teenage daughter?"

"Of course not."

"Well," Fred said, "neither would Bob."

What's a man's definition of true love?

A hard-on.

The newlyweds walked up to the hotel desk and told the clerk, "We just got married this morning and we'd like a room."

"Congratulations," the clerk said. He looked at his list of rooms, then said, "How about the bridle?"

"No, thanks," the groom said, "I'll just hold her ears 'til I get the hang of it."

What's more profitable, a one-story whorehouse or a two-story whorehouse?

A one-story whorehouse—there's not fucking overhead.

What book title best describes sex with your wife?

The Naked and the Dead.

A guy asked his friends to meet him in the bar one night. After a couple drinks, he said, "I have something to confess. You think of me as just one of the guys. But I've really been living a life of torture, because I think of myself as a woman trapped in a man's body. Tomorrow I'm going in for a sex change operation."

The friends were stunned, but they finally managed to wish him good luck. Three months passed, and the friends received another invitation to go to the bar. There was an awkward silence when they encountered a somewhat attractive brunette in a red dress. But after a few drinks, the friends loosened up enough to ask, "How bad was the operation? Did it hurt when they put in those breast implants?"

The newly created woman said, "It hurt some, but not much."

Another guy asked, "I can't even imagine someone cutting off my dick and my balls. That must have been torture."

She replied, "It *did* hurt, but it wasn't the worst."

"What was the worst part of becoming a woman?"

She said, "It was when they had to take out half my brain."

How do you know your wife is really ugly?

You take her to a plastic surgeon and all he can do is graft on a tail.

_____

Did you hear about the new edition of *Playboy* that's directed exclusively at married men?

The centerfold is the same month after month after month.

_____

What's a midwife?

Some one you marry between your first wife and your third wife.

Why is a bottle of beer better than sex with your wife?

Afterwards, a beer bottle is still worth 5 cents.

Why is a bottle of beer better than your wife?

You can enjoy a beer every day of the month.

Why is a bottle of beer better than your wife?

Beer doesn't get jealous when you grab another one.

Why is a bottle of beer better than your wife?

With beer, you always get good head.

———————

Why is a bottle of beer better than your wife?

Beer is always wet.

———————

Why is a bottle of beer better than your wife?

The more frigid the beer, the better.

Why is a bottle of beer better than your wife?

You don't have to wash a beer before it tastes good.

_____

Why is a bottle of beer better than your wife?
A beer doesn't care when you come.

_____

Why is a bottle of beer better than your wife?

If a beer goes flat, you can throw it out.

Why is a bottle of beer better than your wife?

You always know you're the first one to pop a beer.

———————————

A real loser was undressing in the locker room when a friend noticed his dick was all red and chapped. The friend asked, "You've been fucking a girl with a really rough pussy?"

"Nah," the loser said, holding up his palms. "It's calloused hands."

———————————

How do you know your date is a real loser?

You suggest oral sex and he goes home to phone you.

How can you tell if a guy is a real loser?

He calls his penis "Mother."

_____

When do opposites attract?

When he's got insomnia and she's got nympho-mania.

_____

What's it called when you gag on a penis?

The dick-ups.

The husband and wife were arguing about sex when he said, "Other people think a lot of my virility. Why just the other day, I was invited to star in a porn film."

"I believe it," the wife said. "But it would have been a short feature."

———————

Why is prostitution immune to economic fluctuations?

You get laid *on* more than you get laid *off*, and you can always stretch your supply to meet demand.

Chapter Ten:

Simply Disgusting

The man and woman had been having problems in bed, and they finally made an appointment to see a sex therapist. But on the day of the appointment, only the woman showed up.

"Where's your husband?" the therapist asked.

The woman said, "We had a fight a little while ago. He finally said he'd rather go down to the bus station and pick up a stinking, disease-infected whore than talk about having sex with me."

"So where is he?" the therapist repeated.

The woman said, "He's at the bus station."

The old maid walked into the doctor's office and said, "Doctor, you have to help me. I've got a cucumber stuck up my vagina."

The doctor asked, "How long ago did that happen?"

"Last weekend."

The doctor was shocked. "Last weekend? How come you didn't come in until today?"

The old maid said, "I wasn't hungry."

How can you tell a hooker specializes in golden showers?

She's got "Super Soaker" stenciled on her halter top.

A guy walked into a bar and grimaced in great pain as he lowered himself onto a stool. A friend said, "Ed, you look like you should be going to the doctor."

"I already went," Ed said. "I had an appointment on Friday. I've been having some trouble getting it up, and I wanted some pills to stimulate the old gland."

"So what happened?"

"That quack gave me something that backfired. Now I've got the world's biggest hemorrhoids!"

What's the best way to tell an edible mushroom from a poisonous mushroom?

If you wake up the next morning, it's an *edible* mushroom.

Why are men so enthusiastic about the contraceptive sponge?

After they get done fucking the bitch, she can get up and do the dishes.

_____

What's the Polish definition of "liquid asset?"

Diarrhea.

_____

The doctor came into the waiting room and told the man, "Congratulations. You're the father of a brand new baby boy. But I also have to tell you something strange—he was born with a black eye."

The father shrugged, "I guess it's my fault—I got horny on the way to the hospital."

The young girl dropped off her panties at the laundromat with the rest of her clothes. Pinned to the panties was a note that read, "Dear Sir, please use Ultra Tide with Bleach."

The next day, her panties came back with a note pinned to them. It read, "Dear Madam, please use toilet paper."

———————————

A woman opened the door to find a grotesque looking young man standing on the doorstep. She was about to call the police when he called out, "Are you the Mrs. Wilson who had an abortion twenty years ago?"

She turned, blushed, and said, "Yes, I am. How did you know?"

He ignored the question, asking, "And did your boyfriend throw the fetus in the town dump?"

Embarrassed, she mumbled, "Why, yes."

The hideous young man opened his arms and said, "Hi, Mom!"

A guy went to the doctor and said, "Doc, you've got to help me. I've got such a terrible cough I can't sleep a wink all night."

The doctor said, "Take an entire bottle of Ex-Lax."

"Ex-Lax?" the guy repeated. "How can that help me?"

"You'll be to terrified to cough."

————————

What's a cotton picker?

A girl who loses the string on her Tampax.

The mother left the living room one day to get some tea when her little boy came up to her friend and said, "Mrs. Schneider, I'd really like to get into your pants."

The woman blushed furiously. "Why . . . why Jason, what makes you say something that rude."

"Because," he replied, "I shit in mine."

———————

What goes "Puff, thump, squish?"

A jogger stepping in shit.

———————

How can you tell if a Polack's had anal sex?

There's shit on his nose.

How can you tell if a guy is a real loser?

His hobby is saving his ear wax.

———————

What's the only thing more dangerous than swimming in piranha-infested waters?

Doing "69" in Mexico.

———————

Did you hear about the gay necrophiliac?

He liked to fuck people's ashes.

———————

Why do elephants throw up after every shit?

You'd throw up, too, if you had to wipe your ass with your nose.

What goes faster than a rabbit in a field?

A rabbit in a blender.

———————

Why is it so dangerous to French kiss with an epileptic girl?

She might swallow *your* tongue, too.

———————

Did you hear about the new doll for child molesters?

It's called the Ravage Patch Doll.

The world's best hypnotist was appearing at Madison Square Garden. He had his watch at the end of a long chain, swinging it back and forth and saying, "You're all in my power. You're all in my power."

Twenty thousand people went into a deep trance. The hypnotist called out, "You're chickens."

Immediately, the entire crowd started saying, "Cluck, cluck, cluck," and flapping their arms.

"You're roosters," the hypnotist ordered. The crowd immediately switched into "Cock-a-doodle-dos."

The hypnotist was about to give a third command when he suddenly dropped his watch. It shattered on the stage and he exclaimed "Shit!"

It took a week to dig out the crowd.

What do people into golden showers like for lunch?

Pee soup.

_____

What's more disgusting than a golden shower?

A brown bath.

_____

Did you hear about the new V.D. film they're using in elementary schools?

It's called "See Dick Run."

_____

How does a whore know when to stop giving a golden shower?

When she looks down and sees her john is flushed.

How can you tell a baby wasn't wanted?

When it's born with a coat hanger stuck up its ass.

What do you call a fart that comes forth from a dead body?

A stiff wind.

What's another difference between a pig and a pervert?

A pig won't change her panties until a pervert offers to buy them.

What's Polish instant pudding?

An enema.

What does a necrophiliac call closing time at the mortuary?

Happy Hour.

_____

Where do necrophiliacs go on vacation?

Death Valley.

_____

Why are necrophiliacs so unhappy?

The women in their lives are usually rottin'.

_____

What did the necrophiliac get his girlfriend for Christmas?

A Gucci body bag.

How does a child molester make cole slaw?

By creaming in a Cabbage Patch Doll.

———————

When do necrophiliacs play hard ball?

When the corpse has rigor mortis.

———————

Why can you always get a blowjob from a baby?

A baby will put anything in its mouth.

———————

Why did the pizza man rub meatballs on his wife's cunt?

He'd run out of anchovies.

What's grosser than having your girlfriend pass you her gum when you French kiss?

When she tells you she's not chewing gum.

_____

What's the definition of an elegant street walker?

One whose shade of lipstick exactly matches the color of the sores on her mouth.

_____

Why was the whore with V.D. so worn out?

All she ever did was eat and run.

_____

What's the fastest way to have an abortion?

Masturbate with a python.

How do you get invited to a necrophiliac orgy?

You get an in-grave invitation.

———————

What are two fingers to a girl with bulimia?

Dessert.

———————

Did you hear about the do-it-yourself Polish Sex Change Kit?

A blond wig, two falsies, and a meat cleaver.